THE WEST PIER

HUGO WILLIAMS

NEW WALK EDITIONS
Leicester & Nottingham

Acknowledgements

Some of these poems have appeared in the *Times Literary Supplement*, the *London Review of Books* and the *New Statesman*. I would like to thank William Wootten and Nick Everett for their editorial help.

978-1-8381153-6-4

Published by New Walk Editions
c/o Rory Waterman
Nottingham Creative Writing Hub,
Nottingham Trent University, NG11 8NS
and
c/o Nick Everett, Centre for New Writing,
University of Leicester, LE1 7RH

www.newwalkmagazine.com

Printed by imprintdigital, Upton Pyne, Exeter.

Contents

Leaving Faces *5*
Raleigh Street *6*
Pause for Thought *8*
Probably Poor Later *9*
A Brilliant Trick *10*
i.m. Tara Browne *11*
Death Letter *13*
Artist and Model *14*
Virgin *15*
Them *16*
Lapse *17*
Heartbreakfast *18*
Somewhere Else *19*
The Moths *20*
I Don't Know, Sir *21*
Pennies from Heaven *22*
Undiscovered Countries *23*
i.m. The West Pier *24*

Leaving Faces

They turn to look back at me
like riders on a golden galloper,
their smiles in half-profile.

They were going places then,
setting off into the blue
without a care in the world,

but they never arrived there,
only hovered in mid-air,
their smiles losing definition.

With what bright eyes
I studied those leaving faces,
now blasted and frail.

With what shocked innocence
they sway to and fro
on the gibbet memory.

Their lives are shorter now,
their laughter lost
in the clatter of things falling.

Leaving faces never left home,
they hung about upstairs,
watching time fly by

to the sound of fairground music.
No longer dangerous or young,
they are strangely genial,

glazed in otherworldliness,
like hunting trophies of themselves,
shrunken heads on sticks.

I bump into one of them occasionally
with a drink in my hand
and mutter an apology.

Raleigh Street
i.m. Sir Walter Raleigh (1552-1618)

The grim-faced guardian of our street
stands all day in the doorway
of the house opposite,
glaring at everyone who passes.

His job is making sure the sun never shines
on his side of Raleigh Street.
He holds out his hand for rain
and storm clouds gather to his cause.

I spoke to him once
about some misdirected mail I'd received,
saying my own mail sometimes went astray
to nearby Raleigh Mews.

Did he know that Sir Walter
had a concession on alehouses in the area?
I found myself rambling on
about my long-time hero, explaining

how one of the original fireplaces
of the Old Queen's Head in Essex Road
survives in the present-day pub.
I liked to imagine the poet

leaning there, smoking a pipe of Virginia.
There was surely no truth in the legend
that someone threw a pint over him,
thinking he was on fire?

Not a flicker from the bad weather man.
He held out his hand for rain
and a few indifferent drops
showed their contempt for my blow-in.

"It used to be called Thomas Street
before the war," he snarled.
"You can still see the old name
painted on the brickwork over there."

Pause for Thought

My eyes are cast down,
as if from modesty or embarrassment.
My half-closed hands
lie on the table in front of me
where I can see them.

From the way I am sitting,
staring at a sheet of paper,
something would seem to be the matter.
Perhaps I am ill?
Or the temperature of my pen won't come down?

I lean over myself
with a concerned expression on my face,
as if I am visiting.
I think of something kind to say.
My pen moves over the paper for a moment

like the needle of an instrument
for recording brain-life.
From the other side of the street
I look like someone writing.
My head comes up, as if I am pausing to think.

Probably Poor Later

No more getting better.
No more waking up one morning
feeling like your old self again.
Let's call what's-her-name!
See what's going on!
None of that anymore.
No more hitting the street
with a spring in your step
and your knee all right.
Don't even think about it.

You'd like to go out of course,
to see if you still exist,
but you can't obey yourself now,
it hurts too much.
You sit in your chair all day
turning a funny colour.
Where's that list you made?
Someone takes you by the arm
and says how well you're looking.
You haven't changed a bit!

A Brilliant Trick

Being well is such a brilliant trick
with all its happy healthy fun.
Nobody likes you when you're sick.

They think you're being melodramatic
trying to divert attention
from their own habitual trick

of appearing busy and energetic
all the time, so that no one
suspects them of being sick.

They can't imagine your chronic
ill health and depression
are anything more than a cheap trick

to make people more sympathetic
to your phoney mental condition
with its outward signs of being sick.

All you can do is try to mimic
the way healthy people carry on.
Being well is a useful trick.
Everyone hates you when you're sick.

i.m. Tara Browne (1945–1966)

'I read the news today, oh boy,
about a lucky man who made the grade.'
              The Beatles, 'A Day in the Life'

London had barely started
when you blew into town
with your charmed existence,
your cursed Lotus Elan.
You asked me once if I wanted to drive
and we changed places for a moment.
"Come on, Hugo, put your foot down!"
I touched the accelerator
and the thing took off like a bird
down the King's Road.
I don't know where we were going
because I got out and walked.

You entered the 1964
Mercantile Credit Trophy, Formula Three,
but officials found fault
with your windscreen,
which wasn't laminated.
You knocked it through with your elbow
and turned your jacket back to front
to counter the headwind.
You won by three seconds,
"the sensation of the meeting" (*Autosport*).
It was the first lap
of your race to oblivion.

For a couple of multi-coloured years,
while *Help* turned into *Revolver*,
life got in the way.
Your friend Brian Jones
was the prophet of your fate.
With identical blond pageboy
and Cheshire cat grin,
he was your pint-sized twin in negative.
He even managed to roll
his turquoise E-type
but escaped unhurt
with his sickly glow intact.

From *Out of Our Heads* to *Aftermath*,
you parked your pretty car
outside the Scotch or Ad Lib,
while the world dished out its favours
to a lucky few
who could dance all night
and sleep it off next day.
You danced on the accelerator.
You didn't notice that the lights had changed,
but spun the car around
to protect your girlfriend
and went to face the music on your own.

Death Letter

You trusted me with the boy
and now he's gone. What can I say?
That it won't happen again?
That I'll make it up to you?
I'd have given my right arm
to send him home to you in one piece
but someone up there
must have taken a liking
to the boy with sticking-out ears.
Now he's teaching the angels
how to dance the Charleston,
kicking up his heels
on a minefield in heaven.

God knows, it's a hard apprenticeship,
dying for your country
in this tropical paradise,
dancing for a dinner of hot lead.
Our boy must have ordered a drum-roll
of machine-gun fire
before taking his last bow.
We're all of us dying like flies
on this holiday of a lifetime.
The graveyard is fully booked!
It won't be long
till I'm kicking up my heels
on that dance floor in heaven.

Artist and Model

When two heads came together
that should have stayed apart
and two birds of a feather
were shot down by love's dart
the picture seemed to falter
in the looking glass of art.

There was something left unpainted
or something left unsaid
that showed a perfect stranger
in the light the candle shed
that used to look so like her
until they went to bed.

Virgin
from Mallarmé's 'Herodiade'

My hair is no bunch of lilies
stuck in a funeral urn
for the approval of the angels.

It laps my body in hot smells
as if some animal breathed on me.
It mocks my garment's stale chastity.

I lie here stiff with horror at its caresses
until I am half in love
with the shock my hair inspires.

It thrills and frightens me.
It makes me whole. I'll live forever
in the listless wreckage of my innocence.

I'll stand alone on this monotonous earth
and feel on my useless flesh
the sunset's clammy touch.

Wrapped in my scented shroud,
I'll crouch like a reptile on my parchment bed,
swaying my neck to and fro,

while in the glass my hair's metallic sheen
hoards my nakedness from the world
and wild beasts howl...

Them

You can tell from the way they inhabit
time, their relationship with the air,
their contempt for gravity,
that they are not of this world.
They might be an alien species,
these interventions from above,
neither woman nor man exactly,
and not quite animals, alas,
but rainbows made flesh,
an inspiration dressed in light.
Even as they turn their heads
to grant us an audience with the sun
we know they were created elsewhere
and will be going back there without us.

Lapse

However much more polite
it would have been
to leave her body at home
when she went out,

she was obliged to take it with her
everywhere she went
and people in the street
couldn't help noticing this.

Heartbreakfast

I seem to have broken my heart.
I was carrying it upstairs on a tray
like a piece of conceptual art,
when I slipped and broke my heart.
You were playing the critical part.
I knew what you would say:
"If you don't want to break your heart,
don't bring it to me on a tray."

Somewhere Else

I found myself somewhere else,
up north and over to the left.
I was given a new name
and told to sit still.
All my things were on a shelf,
including my cars.
If you loosened one of the screws
they fell on the floor.

I was so far away from home
I hardly existed.
I was a distant memory,
a little old man of seven,
forgetful and quiet.
I sat with my back to the wall.
"Is your mother a prostitute, Williams?"
I said I didn't know.

I taught myself to write in about a week,
remembering things
and hiding them with my arm.
"How is my bike? How is Sam?
Don't let Sam ride my bike."
My handwriting unwound
like the slow-moving wire
of the fire escape mechanism,

screaming for help
as it lowered me to the ground
on Fire Practice Day.
Everyone was shouting my name,
telling me where to put my feet
when I got stuck in the ivy.
A photo of me crying
appeared in the school magazine.

The Moths

"Don't worry, darling, three months
will soon fly past, you'll see.
Then you'll be coming home again
to your own little room upstairs."

Every night I watched
the poor blind things flying past,
burning their papery wings
on the strip lighting of the dormitory.

I Don't Know, Sir

When they catch us red-handed,
flicking ink pellets in class,
passing notes behind their backs,
they always ask the same question:
what do we think we're doing
and who is responsible for this mess?
When they take us by the ear
and ask who we think we are
and when are we going to grow up,
we can only think of one answer.

When they ask us quietly, man to man,
how we plan to earn a living
if we never listen in class,
we find ourselves searching the horizon
for a life in the real world
and have to admit we don't know.
When they catch us out of bounds,
and ask where we think we're going,
smoking and wearing the wrong shoes,
we answer truthfully enough.

Pennies from Heaven

Spots of Leichner "5" and "9"
alternate round my father's face like warpaint
in his dressing-room mirror.
He rubs them down to a healthy tan
for the part of Julian
in "We at the Crossroads" at Her Majesty's.
Next morning, dressed to kill
in government-issue busman's overcoat,
long in the sleeve
(white arm-band for "Officer Material"),
he finds himself drilling
with other actor-volunteers
in the Queen's Westminsters,
presenting tightly-furled umbrellas
in the pouring rain.

"Don't just do something, sit there"
is the word of command
to the men guarding Staines Railway Bridge
during the Phoney War.
My father, whose debts to the Inland Revenue
amount to four figures,
receives only eight shillings and sixpence
in his weekly wage packet,
about what it cost him
to look after his top hat before the war.
He has placed the coins on the railway line
and let a train pass over them.
Now they are larger, flatter,
and completely useless,
except as playthings for his son.

Undiscovered Countries

Sun going down with a splash and a hiss
into a silent sea,
words returning with a bang and a bell
to the left-hand margin,
pausing for a moment to reflect on the scene.

Sun lifting its tousled head
out of yesterday's wreckage
washed up on the shore,
words bearing news of undiscovered countries,
sometimes taking us there.

i.m. The West Pier (1866 – 2003)

Piers are stepping-stones
out of this world, a line of poetry
flung out to sea on a whim,
a dazzle of sea lights
glimpsed between floorboards.

For 50p you can study eternity
through a telescope
and never have to go there,
only promenade to nowhere and back
in an atmosphere of ice cream.

We used to take the speedboat ride
between the two piers,
pulling the canvas up to our chins
when the spray flew in our faces.
Now we stand and stare

at the remains of our innocence,
twisted girders piled up
in a heap of dead holidays,
while Brighton limps out to sea
on its one good leg.

*

There it is over there,
a little rusty island moored offshore,
the empty cage of its dome
lying lower in the water
every time I come down.
Where are the luminous dolphins
on the merry-go-round?
Buffalo Bill's Wild West?

They could have saved the old pier,
but they gave it away to the crabs
and put up a giant pogo-stick
on the seafront,
a middle finger to its memory.
Now only seagulls cry
in what's left of the concert hall,
only storms shift the scenery.

It sinks below the horizon,
a black and tangled sunset
surrounded by bubbles.
Madame Esmerelda, gypsy fortune-teller,
presses her lips to the glass
of her waterlogged cubicle
and gurgles her apologies
for getting it all so wrong.